★ ★ ★ ★ ★ ★ ★ ★ ★ ★ ★ ★ ★ ★ ★ ★ ★ ★ ★

U.S. MILITARY DESIGNS for Woodworking & Other Crafts

Completely Revised and Expanded 2nd Edition

Mike and Vicky Lewis

With Designs for Veterans by Dirk Boelman, Judy Gale Roberts, and Steve Westfall

A SCROLL SAW WOODWORKING & CRAFTS BOOK

www.ScrollSawer.com

DEDICATION

MIKE AND VICKY LEWIS

This book is dedicated to all the men and women who have served our country, to the families of those who have served, and to all of the men and women who are currently enlisted.

This book is in loving memory of Mike's uncle, James Phillips, an Army Infantry Veteran and Silver Star recipient from the Vietnam War.

This book is also dedicated to Mike's stepfather, Howard "Doc" Kash, a Navy Veteran from the Korean Conflict and World War II.

U.S. Military Designs for Woodworking & Other Crafts is a revised and updated version of *Scroll Saw Military Designs* (978-1-56523-146-7, 2000). This new edition includes fourteen new patterns and expanded how-to instructions. *United We Stand* was originally published in *Scroll Saw Workshop. Military Tribute Plaque* and one *Veterans Ornament* were originally published in *Scroll Saw Woodworking & Crafts* magazine. The patterns contained herein are copyrighted by the authors. Readers may make copies of these patterns for personal use. The patterns themselves, however, are not to be duplicated for resale or distribution under any circumstances. Any such copying is a violation of copyright law.

Library of Congress Cataloging-in-Publication Data

Lewis, Mike.
  U.S. military designs for woodworking & other crafts / Mike and Vicky Lewis ; with additional designs by Dirk Boelman and others.
    pages cm -- (Scroll saw military designs)
  Includes index.
  ISBN 978-1-56523-869-5
  1. Scrollwork. 2. Woodwork--Patterns. 3. Woodwork--United States--Themes, motives, etc. 4. Military decorations. 5. Military art and science in art. I. Lewis, Vicky. II. Title. III. Title: United States military designs for woodworking & other crafts.
  TT190.6.L49 2015
  745.51'3--dc23
                    2015007419

To learn more about the other great books from Fox Chapel Publishing, or to find a retailer near you, call toll-free 800-457-9112 or visit us at *www.FoxChapelPublishing.com*.

Note to Authors: We are always looking for talented authors to write new books. Please send a brief letter describing your idea to Acquisition Editor, 1970 Broad Street, East Petersburg, PA 17520.

Printed in the United States of America
First printing

EDITOR'S NOTE

When the first edition of *Scroll Saw Military Designs* came out in 2000, there was nothing like it available. Here was a book that allowed you to create custom plaques for family or friends who served or were serving in the U.S. Armed Services.

For this new revised edition, we've redrawn all of the original hand-drawn patterns to create crisp and thin lines. We've shaded them to make it easy to see what to cut and when. And we've added a few missing specialties, such as the U.S. Army Corps of Engineers. We've also included patterns to create custom plaques for veterans of all of the major conflicts between World War I and Operation Enduring Freedom and Operation Iraqi Freedom.

We've added the late Dirk Boelman's Christmas ornament patterns for veterans. We've also included the United We Stand plaque by Judy Gale Roberts in honor of September 11, as well as a customizable memorial picture frame pattern from Steve Westfall, both originally published in *Scroll Saw Woodworking & Crafts*.

It is our hope that you will use these plaques to honor the men and women who have served or are currently serving in the Armed Services.

—Bob Duncan

A Note about Non-Commercial Use

Since the publication of *Scroll Saw Military Designs*, the United States government has trademarked the Department of Defense and Military Seals to prevent companies from using them to imply the Military Services were endorsing a company or product. The trademark also prevents companies from profiting from printing apparel with the military insignia that requires licensing fees. Basically, the trademark is intended to keep people from profiting from and/or disrespecting the insignia. However, if you are making the designs for your family, friends, or yourself, there should be no issues. For more information, visit www.defense.gov/trademarks/.

CONTENTS

PLAQUE PATTERNS

ADDITIONAL PROJECTS

About the Authors

MIKE AND VICKY LEWIS

Mike Lewis, an Army veteran, has been perfecting his scroll saw techniques since 1987. What started as a hobby for Mike became a rewarding career, progressing from basic scrollwork projects to creating his own designs and teaching.

Vicky began scrolling in 1998 to help Mike, and it quickly became a passion for her. Cutting almost daily, she quickly realized the scroll saw could be used not only to cut elegant Victorian scrollwork, but also to cut the many wood items and personal designs they have on display.

DIRK BOELMAN

The late Dirk Boelman got hooked on scrolling with the first project he cut in 1987. Drawing patterns always came naturally to him, and his work appears in numerous books, magazines, and other publications around the world. Dirk's love for scroll sawing was matched only by his passion for honoring veterans, and these two callings blossomed into Dirk's Scroll Sawing for Veterans program. For more of Dirk's work, visit www.TheArtFactory.com.

JUDY GALE ROBERTS

Judy Gale Roberts, born in Houston, Tex., has long been recognized as the leading authority on intarsia. Judy was one of the first ten people to be inducted into the Woodworking Hall of Fame. For more of her work or information on classes held at her home studio in Seymour, Tenn., contact Judy at 800-316-9010, or visit www.intarsia.com. Judy's numerous intarsia books are available at www.FoxChapelPublishing.com.

STEVE WESTFALL

Steve Westfall was raised in the very small community of New Creek, WV on about 500 acres of woodland. He got his appreciation for wood from his father, who was a carpenter for the B&O Railroad. In 1991, he was asked to create some crafts for a special needs class to decorate. He bought a scroll saw and fell in love with the craft. He began to design some of his own patterns, and particularly enjoys designing portraits and custom frames. Steven Westfall lives in Arthur, WV. Contact him via email at steve03@frontiernet.net.

GETTING STARTED

Selecting Materials

These plaques are made from a single piece of ¼" (6mm)-thick wood with sections elevated using spacers. You can make the plaques from nearly any hardwood or plywood but pine. Pine can be difficult to stain without becoming blotchy and is often too soft for delicate fretwork. For strength and stability, use ⅛" (3mm)- and ¼" (6mm)-thick plywood for the spacers and backing boards.

Working with Patterns

Start by photocopying or scanning the original into a computer. You can use the copier or photo-editing software to adjust the size of the final pattern to fit the blank (the wood for the project). Then, to cut a plaque, you'll need to attach the pattern to the blank. There are several easy ways to do this.

- Spray adhesive or glue stick: Cover the wood with painter's tape, which will lubricate the saw blade and make it easy to peel the pattern off. Apply spray adhesive or a glue stick to the back of the pattern and smooth the pattern onto the tape. Cover the pattern with clear packing tape, if desired; this also helps to lubricate the blade.

- Shelf paper: Apply spray adhesive or a glue stick to the back of the pattern, and smooth the pattern onto the shiny side of the shelf paper. Cut the pieces apart, if necessary, peel the paper backing off the shelf paper, and stick the pattern to the wood. The shelf paper both lubricates the blade and is easy to remove from the wood.

Selecting Blades

For these designs, we use a #5 reverse-tooth blade for the large open areas, a #2 reverse-tooth blade for the tighter areas, and a #2/0 blade for the tightest letters and vein lines. Some folks prefer a #2/0 spiral reverse-blade for the tiny lettering and veining cuts. The reverse-tooth blades prevent tear out on the bottom of the blank and reduces the amount of sanding you will have to do later.

Stacking the Pieces

Depending on the thickness of your material, stacking at least two blanks together will protect delicate fretwork, speed up your production, and, especially if you're cutting thin blanks, increase your cutting accuracy. There are several methods to secure a stack of blanks. The most important part: making sure the pattern is on top of the stack.

- Tape: Align the layers and wrap a layer of tape around the outside edge. You can also wrap the whole stack with tape for extra stability. Scrollers can use either masking tape, painter's tape, or clear packaging tape.

- Hot glue: Glue the blanks together with a glob of hot-melt glue on each corner, or cover all four edges of the stack with glue. Avoid placing glue in areas that will be part of the project.

- Brads: Drive small brads or nails into the four corners of the stacked blanks. A brad nailer (pneumatic, electric, or battery-powered) makes this easy. If you plan to drive the nails by hand, I suggest drilling pilot holes just smaller than the diameter of the brads to keep from splitting the wood. Be sure to cut off any overhanging nails as close to the surface as you can, and then sand them flush to avoid scratching or catching on the saw table.

Blade-entry Holes

Drill a vertical hole as marked. Use a drill press if you have one; angled holes may interfere with delicate fretwork. Drill through the blank into scrap wood to prevent tear-out on the back of the blank. If you have the space, use a larger drill bit—it will make it easier to thread the blades through. For thin veining cuts, use the smallest bit the blade will fit through.

Making the Plaques

CUTTING THE PATTERNS

Start by cutting the 7" (178mm)-diameter circle for the backing board and four small rectangular ⅛" (3mm)-thick and four small rectangular ¼" (6mm)-thick plywood spacers. The plaques are cut from a single piece of wood in a specific order. Use the drawing below as a guide to plan your cuts.

1. Cut the delicate frets in the middle and work your way out.

2. Cut the letters and stars.

3. Cut the inner ring.

4. Cut the center ring.

5. Cut the outer ring. Cut in a counterclockwise direction on the line between the middle ring and the outer ring. Then, go back and cut the detail veining lines to make the outer ring look like rope.

6. Cut the perimeter. Cut the perimeter in three sections so you can keep the stack secured for as long as possible. Start in the top center and cut clockwise to bottom center, and then cut the excess scrap free. Go back and cut the veining details on the first exposed half. Then, cut all but the last inch or so of the remaining half, and cut the excess scrap free. Cut the veining details on the exposed area. Then, cut the perimeter and veining details as you cut the remaining section of the ring. Hold the blanks together tightly as you make the last cuts, which will free the stack.

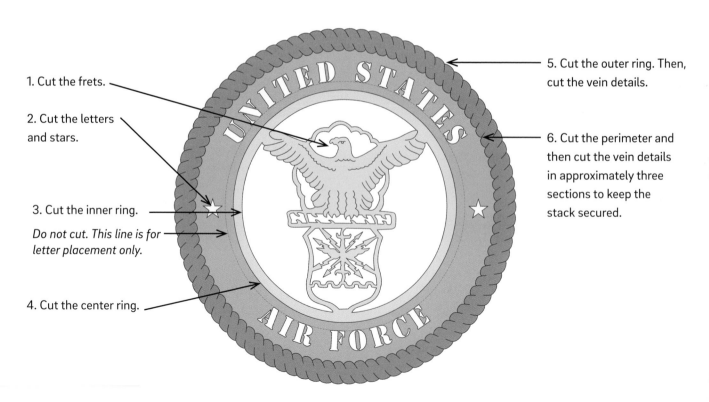

1. Cut the frets.

2. Cut the letters and stars.

3. Cut the inner ring.

Do not cut. This line is for letter placement only.

4. Cut the center ring.

5. Cut the outer ring. Then, cut the vein details.

6. Cut the perimeter and then cut the vein details in approximately three sections to keep the stack secured.

FINISHING THE PLAQUES

To remove the pattern, use a commercial adhesive remover or dampen the pattern with mineral spirits. A quick wipe of mineral spirits removes most adhesives left behind on the wood. Allow the wood to dry, and then stain or dye the different rings for contrast. Paint or dye the backing board as desired. Allow the finish to dry.

GLUE SELECTION

For this project, I suggest you use ordinary wood glue or cyanoacrylate (CA) glue such as Super Glue™. Wood glue gives you more time to position the spacers and rings properly, but it also takes longer to dry. Clean up wood glue with soap and water, and scrape off any glue squeeze out with a sharp blade.

CA glue sets up fast, but it reduces the time you have to position the spacers and rings properly. It also bonds skin as easily as wood, so if you do use CA glue, be careful that you don't attach your fingers to the wood when positioning the small spacers. You can remove CA glue using acetone or special CA glue debonder. If you position the pieces incorrectly, a careful but sharp rap against a hard surface can sometimes break the CA glue joint.

ASSEMBLING THE PLAQUES

Place the backing board face up on the bench. Apply glue to the back of the outer ring, center it on the backing board, making sure the backing board is not visible through the veining details on the outer edge of the ring, and clamp or hold it securely until the glue sets. Then glue and clamp or hold the ⅛" (3mm)-thick spacers to the back of the center ring. Position the spacers so they will not be visible through the frets. When the glue has set, apply glue to the backs of the spacers, and carefully glue and clamp or hold the center ring to the backing board. Repeat the process with the ¼" (6mm)-thick spacers for the inner ring. After the glue dries, seal the project with a few coats of spray finish, such as lacquer. A lacquer finish also disguises any CA glue squeeze out. Then, attach a hanger to the back if desired.

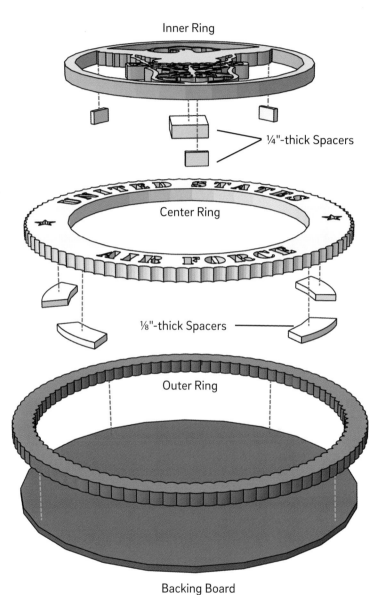

Inner Ring

¼"-thick Spacers

Center Ring

⅛"-thick Spacers

Outer Ring

Backing Board

UNITED STATES AIR FORCE VETERAN

AIR FORCE
★ ★ ★

UNITED STATES
AIR FORCE RETIRED

ARMY

ARMY

NATIONAL GUARD

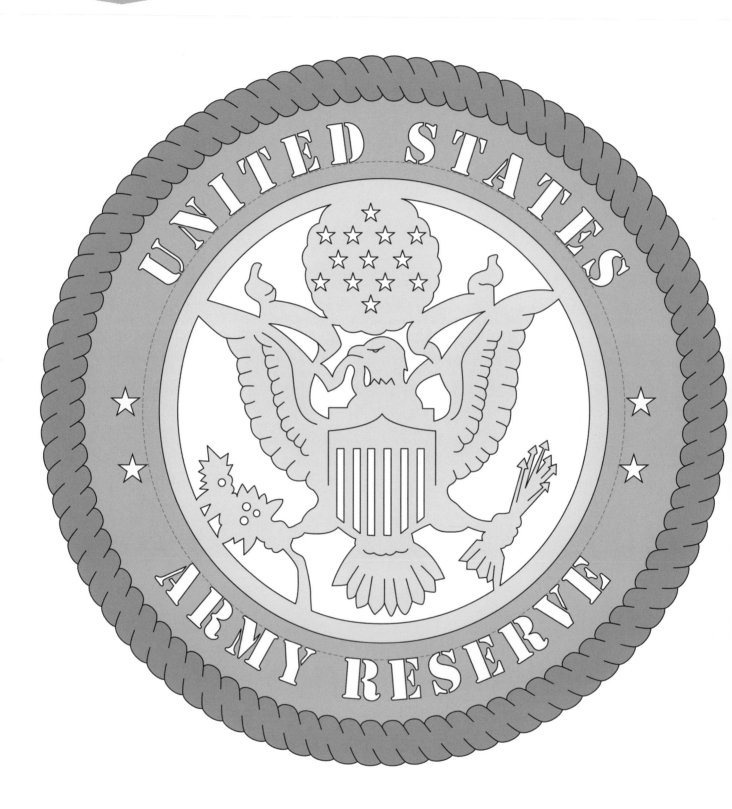

ARMY

UNITED STATES ARMY RESERVE

UNITED STATES

ARMY RECRUITER

UNITED STATES

ARMY AIR CORPS

ARMY

UNITED STATES ARMY SPECIAL FORCES

SPECIAL FORCES

AIRBORNE

U.S. SPECIAL FORCES

GREEN BERET

DE OPPRESSO LIBER

Note: We suggest woodburning or writing the words "Semper Fidelis" because they would be very difficult to cut.

Note: We suggest woodburning or writing the words "Semper Fidelis" because they would be very difficult to cut.

Note: We suggest woodburning or writing the words "Semper Fidelis" because they would be very difficult to cut.

Note: We suggest woodburning or writing the words "Semper Fidelis" because they would be very difficult to cut.

Note: We suggest woodburning or writing the words "Semper Fidelis" because they would be very difficult to cut.

Note: We suggest woodburning or writing the words "Semper Fidelis" because they would be very difficult to cut.

UNITED STATES MARINE CORPS

SEMPER FIDELIS

AVIATION

Note: We suggest woodburning or writing the words "Semper Fidelis" because they would be very difficult to cut.

Note: We suggest woodburning or writing the words "Semper Fidelis" because they would be very difficult to cut.

SEMPER FIDELIS

Note: We suggest woodburning or writing the words "Semper Fidelis" because they would be very difficult to cut.

UNITED STATES NAVY

RESERVE

U.S. MILITARY DESIGNS For Woodworking and Other Crafts

UNITED STATES NAVAL AVIATION

U.S. NAVY SEABEE

RETIRED

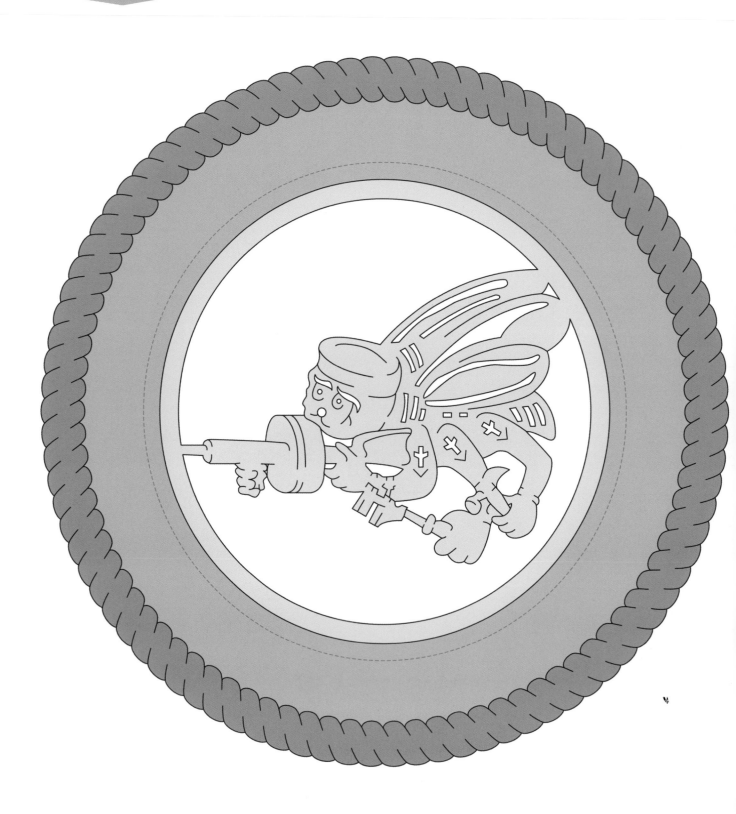

Lettering and Customization

Use the words, seals, and blank rope ring design in this section to create your own designs for veterans of foreign wars. For example, "Desert Storm Veteran" can be placed around any of the six seals on the following pages. Using this method, you can easily create veteran plaques for Army, Air Force, Coast Guard, Marine Corps, Navy, or Navy Seabee for each of the major conflicts since World War I. Or, use the provided alphabet and numbers on the blank rope ring design to further customize the patterns.

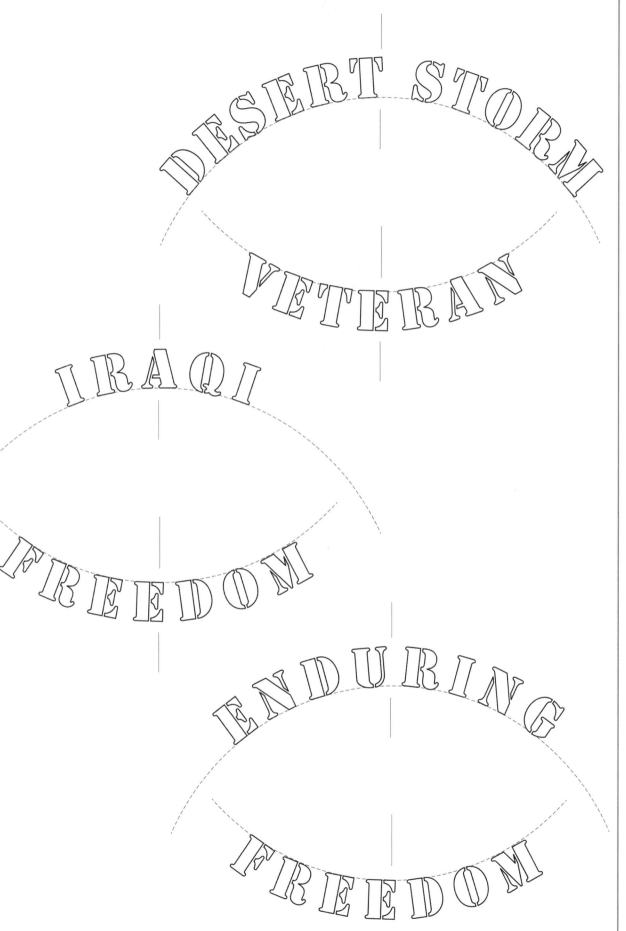

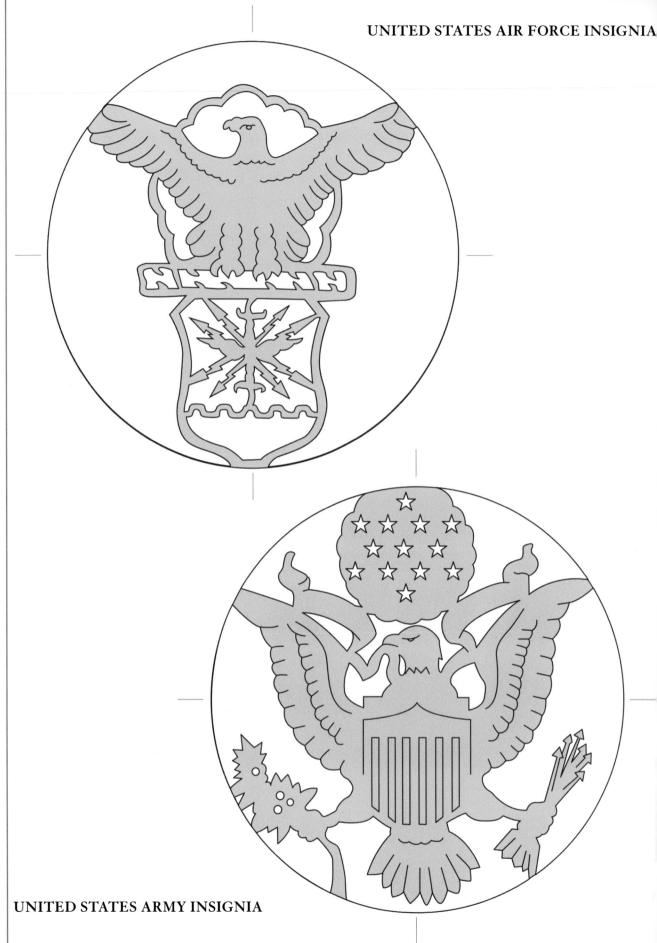

UNITED STATES ARMY INSIGNIA

UNITED STATES COAST GUARD INSIGNIA

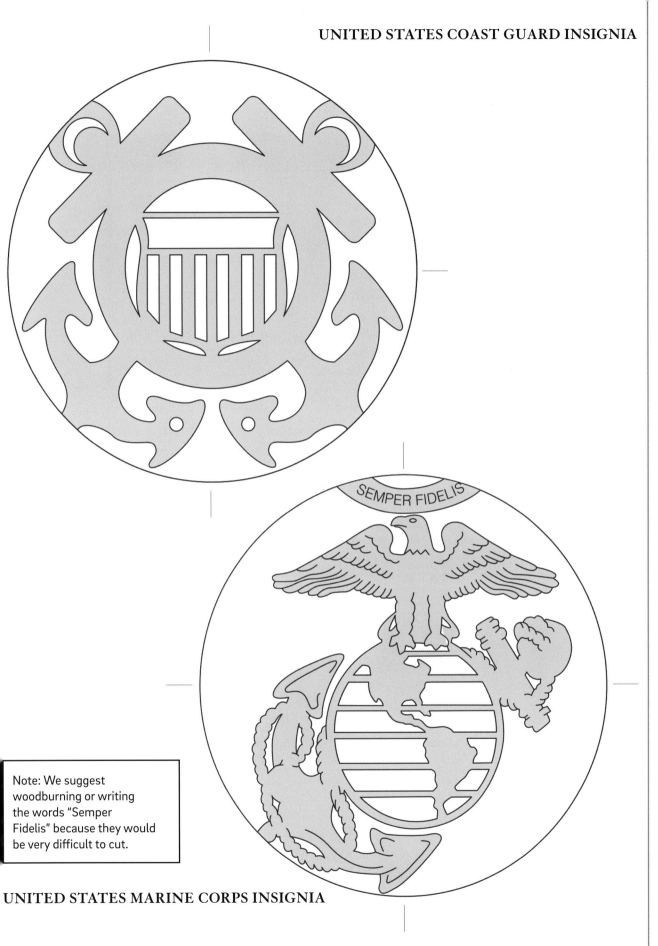

Note: We suggest woodburning or writing the words "Semper Fidelis" because they would be very difficult to cut.

UNITED STATES MARINE CORPS INSIGNIA

UNITED STATES NAVY SEABEE INSIGNIA

John W. Parsons U S ARMY

Military Tribute Plaque

BY STEVE WESTFALL

Support the men and women in uniform with this plaque honoring your hometown heroes. You can stack-cut several soldier portraits at one time and then personalize each plaque with the individual's name, rank, and dates of service.

Cut the blank to fit your frame; I use an 11" by 17" (279mm by 432mm) frame. Position the pattern for the soldier to one side, and cut the fretwork. Then, mark and cut the opening for the frame. Copy the letters you need to personalize the design, and draw guidelines on the blank to help you position the letters properly. Cut the letters and remove any fuzzies. Add the photo, and attach a black backing board before inserting the project in a frame.

ABCDEFGHIJ

KLMNOPQR

STUVWXYZ

abcdefghij

klmnopqr

stuvwxyz

1234567890

U.S. MILITARY DESIGNS For Woodworking and Other Crafts

You Are Not Forgotten

In this plaque, the black overlay signifies the punishment and cruelty the soldiers endured as prisoners of war. The white background signifies hope.

To make this plaque, cut the background out of ¾" (19mm)-thick stock. Then, cut the overlay out of ¼" (6mm)-thick stock. Paint the background white and the overlay black. Then, use cyanoacrylate (CA) glue, such as Super Glue™, to attach the overlay centered on the background.

United We Stand

PATTERN DESIGNED BY JUDY GALE ROBERTS

PROJECT CUT BY MIKE AND VICKY LEWIS

To make this design, attach the pattern to the blanks and cut the frets. Use double-sided tape to attach the ¼" (6mm)-thick Baltic birch plywood for the backing, and then cut the perimeter. Stain the fretwork as desired, and paint the backing board with blue and red or use glue sticks to attach appropriate colors of construction paper to the fretwork. Then, glue and clamp the backing board to the fretwork. Apply a clear spray finish to the front of the piece and attach a hanger to the back.

PATTERN SHOWN AT 50%

PATTERN SHOWN AT 50%

Christmas Ornaments

BY DIRK AND KAREN BOELMAN

Start by enlarging or reducing the patterns as desired. If you plan to hang the ornaments on a tree, use ¼" (6mm)-thick or thinner stock. Wood selection and color are personal choices. For a durable ornament, cut it from plywood and paint, stain, or dye it as desired. However, ornaments look best if cut from solid wood. For a green tree (natural or artificial), choose a light wood, such as pine, oak, or aspen. For a white or silver artificial tree, choose a darker wood, such as walnut, mahogany, or cedar.

To protect the fragile fretwork (and to speed your production), cut a stack of blanks (see page 8). I like to cover the top of the stack with painter's tape, attach the pattern to the tape, and then cover the pattern with clear packaging tape. The two tapes lubricate the blades and prevent burning, especially when you're cutting dense hardwoods. The tapes also make it easy to peel the pattern off after you finish cutting.

Drill blade-entry holes as required. Use the smallest bit you can fit the scroll saw blade through for the veining lines, and drill the hole in the widest part of the line, if possible. Use the scroll saw blade to blend the round hole with the rest of the veining line. Use a larger bit for the larger frets. Cut the frets first, and then cut the perimeter of the ornaments. Remove the pattern and use sandpaper or needle files to remove the fuzzies or rough cuts. Apply a finish, and then hang the ornaments with pride.

GOD BLESS OUR NATIONAL GUARD

U.S. COAST GUARD

USMC SEMPER FI

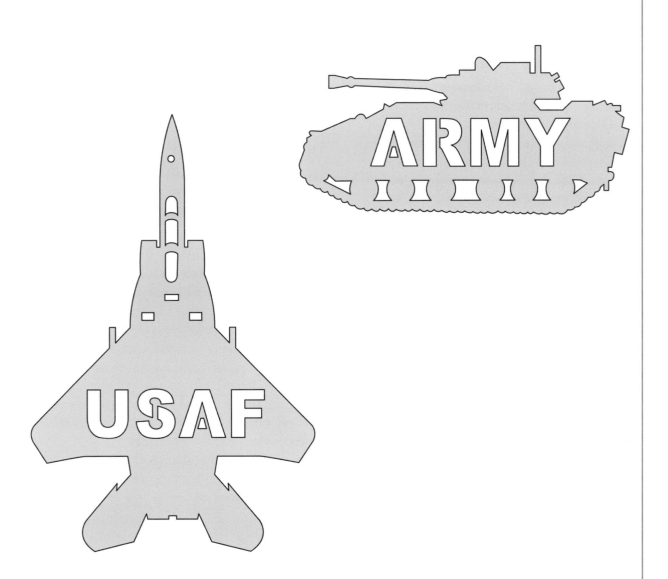

Dirk Boelman's Scroll Sawing for Veterans Program

BY KAREN BOELMAN

Dirk Boelman was passionate about two things: scroll sawing and honoring our veterans. He wanted to combine these passions and create a program that taught veterans the art of scroll sawing. Thus, his Scroll Sawing for Veterans Program was born. Anyone involved in the art form understands how it feels to lose yourself in the project at hand. Scroll sawing occupies your mind and gives you a tremendous sense of accomplishment when a project is completed. It promotes a feeling of pride to create something of beauty with your own hands. Dirk felt this gift, which scroll sawing gives to people in general, would be an especially important gift for veterans. Thus, the Scroll Sawing For Veterans Program began as a desire to teach veterans the art of scroll sawing.

Working through the Veterans Freedom Center in Dubuque, Iowa, Dirk and I began teaching scroll sawing classes to veterans a few years ago. The Veterans Freedom Center is a very special place that provides a shop with several scroll saws and other woodworking machines, plus patterns, wood, and other supplies, free of charge to veterans in Iowa, Illinois, and Wisconsin. It is staffed by a knowledgeable and dedicated group of veterans who are always willing to help someone else get started at scroll sawing. We have witnessed the therapeutic effects of scroll sawing and believe it is the perfect hobby to teach to veterans.

Another part of Dirk's Scroll Sawing for Veterans Program was making and distributing ornaments to thank veterans for their service. These ornament patterns were given free of charge to all scroll sawyers who asked for them. The idea was for scroll sawyers to cut and finish the ornaments, and then distribute them to veterans in their part of the country. We have heard hundreds of heartfelt stories from people who donated the ornaments to church members for Veterans Day and gave them to patients at VA hospitals, honor-flight attendees, veterans groups, National Guard troops returning from deployments, family members, and friends.

The reactions of both the givers and receivers of the ornaments were immensely touching, and we have found it to be a very worthwhile project for all who were involved. We encouraged the scroll sawyers to send any extra ornaments back to us. We distributed them to folks who did not have the ability to cut the ornaments themselves, but wanted to distribute them. We suggested people sign and date the ornaments they scrolled. We included a card with the ornaments we distributed to let each veteran know who created the gift. The card also included our contact information for anyone who wanted to find out more about the program. This part of the program has been very successful, and I would estimate that thousands of ornaments have been distributed through it. Veterans are very touched by this simple act of kindness and recognition.

We were just beginning to organize the final aspect of the Scroll Sawing for Veterans Program when Dirk passed away. We are so lucky to have the Veterans Freedom Center in our area, but that kind of resource is not available everywhere. Dirk wanted to establish a nationwide database to connect potential teachers with potential students. Once this database is established, we will be able to help make those connections and promote the art of scroll sawing to more veterans around the country.

The Scroll Sawing for Veterans Program was a very important part of Dirk's life, and I want to continue the legacy for him. I will continue distributing the ornaments, organizing and teaching classes, and establishing the database for teachers and students. All of this information is on my Art Factory website, although I plan to eventually have an independent website for the program.

If you would like more information or would like to become involved in any aspect of the program, please contact me at www.TheArtFactory.com.

INDEX

Note: Page numbers in *italics* indicate patterns/projects.

INDEX